W9-BPM-124

Part of the "Cuss Words Make Me Happy™" Series of Journals, Planners and Books by Crazy Tired Beetches™.
Visit Crazy Tired Beetches™ online: www.crazytiredbeetches.com | email us: feedback@crazytiredbeetches.com

ISBN: 978-1725628359

Revised edition: Published 12-2018

THIS
Gratitude Journal
BELONGS TO

DATE: 12/27/21

🍍 Asshole of the Day 🍍

Today, I'm Proud I Didn't...

Cry @ the start of my day

Today, I am Happy I Did...

Get my motivation back to work

🍍 I'm Lucky To Have 🍍

My Family
My Friends
Jon
My Job
My motivation

MY MOOD TODAY (RATED IN PINEAPPLES)

🍍 🍍 🍍 🍍 🍍 🍍 🍍 🍍 🍍 🍍 🍍

Today's Shit List
PEOPLE, PLACES OR THINGS

- o Clinic Outreach ?
- o Colombia videography ?
- o IP reach out
- o
- o
- o
- o

Other Shit To Remember

DATE: 2/14/2022

Asshole of the Day

NO ONE!

Today, I'm Proud I Didn't...

Cry
Have to worry about Amina

Today, I am Happy I Did...

Follow up on current cases

I'm Lucky To Have

A business
Friends
Support system

MY MOOD TODAY (RATED IN PINEAPPLES)

DRAW SOME SHIT HERE

♡ I deserve Love

Today's Shit List
PEOPLE, PLACES OR THINGS

- Laura Lee ✓
- Amina Appears ✓
- IP clean up ✓
-
-
-
-
-

Other Shit To Remember

Shantal ?

DATE: 2/21/22

🍍 Asshole of the Day 🍍

Gad Lavy - For acusing me of stealing his donors

Today, I'm Proud I Didn't...

I will NOT be
defined by what he
did/is doing. I will
be so fucking sucessful

Today, I am Happy I Did...

meditated ♡

🍍 I'm Lucky To Have 🍍

Jon
myself
my family

MY MOOD TODAY (RATED IN PINEAPPLES)

🍍 🍍 🍍 🍍 🍍 🍍 🍍 🍍 🍍 🍍 🍍

2/22/22

Orly

- ○ Gad Lavy
- ○
- ○
- ○
- ○
- ○
- ○

Other Shit To Remember

Marketing — Woofie
            — tlk + dc

IP Case Review

308 - AMH ?   285 - AMH ?

306 - testing ?   ORLY - $500

287 - WTF ?   S Address :

246 - pending   Orly flyer in Hebrew

DATE: _____

Asshole of the Day

Today, I'm Proud I Didn't...   Today, I am Happy I Did...

I'm Lucky To Have

MY MOOD TODAY (RATED IN PINEAPPLES)

WRITE YOUR OWN FUCKING QUOTE

Today's Shit List
PEOPLE, PLACES OR THINGS

- ○
- ○
- ○
- ○
- ○
- ○
- ○

Other Shit To Remember

DATE: _____

Asshole of the Day

_____
_____
_____
_____
_____
_____
_____
_____

Today, I'm Proud I Didn't...

_____
_____
_____
_____
_____
_____
_____

Today, I am Happy I Did...

_____
_____
_____
_____
_____
_____
_____

I'm Lucky To Have

_____
_____
_____
_____
_____
_____
_____

MY MOOD TODAY (RATED IN PINEAPPLES)

Today's Shit List
PEOPLE, PLACES OR THINGS

"MAY YOUR DAY GO FAST, YOUR SOCKS MATCH & YOUR UNDERWEAR NOT RIDE UP YOUR ASS."

- ○
- ○
- ○
- ○
- ○
- ○
- ○

Other Shit To Remember

DATE: _____

Asshole of the Day

Today, I'm Proud I Didn't...

Today, I am Happy I Did...

I'm Lucky To Have

MY MOOD TODAY (RATED IN PINEAPPLES)

CAPTURE RANDOM FUCKERY HERE

Today's Shit List
PEOPLE, PLACES OR THINGS

○
○
○
○
○
○
○

Other Shit To Remember

DATE: _____

Asshole of the Day

_____

Today, I'm Proud I Didn't...

Today, I am Happy I Did...

I'm Lucky To Have

MY MOOD TODAY (RATED IN PINEAPPLES)

WRITE YOUR OWN FUCKING QUOTE

Today's Shit List
PEOPLE, PLACES OR THINGS

- ○
- ○
- ○
- ○
- ○
- ○
- ○

Other Shit To Remember

DATE: _____

Asshole of the Day

Today, I'm Proud I Didn't...   Today, I am Happy I Did...

I'm Lucky To Have

MY MOOD TODAY (RATED IN PINEAPPLES)

> **REVENGE IS NOT IN MY PLANS. YOU'LL FUCK YOURSELF ON YOUR OWN.**

- ○
- ○
- ○
- ○
- ○
- ○
- ○

Other Shit To Remember

DATE: _____

Asshole of the Day

_____
_____
_____
_____
_____
_____
_____

Today, I'm Proud I Didn't...   Today, I am Happy I Did...

I'm Lucky To Have

_____
_____
_____
_____
_____
_____
_____
_____

MY MOOD TODAY (RATED IN PINEAPPLES)

DRAW SOME SHIT HERE

Today's Shit List
PEOPLE, PLACES OR THINGS

- ○
- ○
- ○
- ○
- ○
- ○
- ○

Other Shit To Remember

DATE: _____

Asshole of the Day

Today, I'm Proud I Didn't... _Today, I am Happy I Did..._

I'm Lucky To Have

MY MOOD TODAY (RATED IN PINEAPPLES)

CAPTURE RANDOM FUCKERY HERE

Today's Shit List
PEOPLE, PLACES OR THINGS

Other Shit To Remember

DATE: _____

DAY OF THE WEEK
S M T W TH F S

Asshole of the Day

Today, I'm Proud I Didn't...

Today, I am Happy I Did...

I'm Lucky To Have

MY MOOD TODAY (RATED IN PINEAPPLES)

WRITE YOUR OWN FUCKING QUOTE

Today's Shit List
PEOPLE, PLACES OR THINGS

- ○
- ○
- ○
- ○
- ○
- ○
- ○

Other Shit To Remember

DATE: _____

Asshole of the Day

_____
_____
_____
_____
_____
_____
_____
_____

Today, I'm Proud I Didn't...   ### Today, I am Happy I Did...

_____   _____
_____   _____
_____   _____
_____   _____
_____   _____
_____   _____

I'm Lucky To Have

_____
_____
_____
_____
_____
_____
_____

MY MOOD TODAY (RATED IN PINEAPPLES)

Today's Shit List
PEOPLE, PLACES OR THINGS

"CAN YOU SEE THE 'FUCK YOU' IN MY SMILE?"

Other Shit To Remember

DATE: _____

Asshole of the Day

_____
_____
_____
_____
_____
_____
_____
_____

Today, I'm Proud I Didn't...

_____
_____
_____
_____
_____
_____

Today, I am Happy I Did...

_____
_____
_____
_____
_____
_____

I'm Lucky To Have

_____
_____
_____
_____
_____
_____
_____

MY MOOD TODAY (RATED IN PINEAPPLES)

DRAW SOME SHIT HERE

Today's Shit List
PEOPLE, PLACES OR THINGS

- ○
- ○
- ○
- ○
- ○
- ○
- ○

Other Shit To Remember

DATE: _____

Asshole of the Day

_____

Today, I'm Proud I Didn't...   Today, I am Happy I Did...

I'm Lucky To Have

MY MOOD TODAY (RATED IN PINEAPPLES)

CAPTURE RANDOM FUCKERY HERE

Today's Shit List
PEOPLE, PLACES OR THINGS

- ○
- ○
- ○
- ○
- ○
- ○
- ○

Other Shit To Remember

DATE: _____

Asshole of the Day

_____

Today, I'm Proud I Didn't...   Today, I am Happy I Did...

I'm Lucky To Have

_____

MY MOOD TODAY (RATED IN PINEAPPLES)

WRITE YOUR OWN FUCKING QUOTE

Today's Shit List
PEOPLE, PLACES OR THINGS

- ○
- ○
- ○
- ○
- ○
- ○
- ○

Other Shit To Remember

DATE: _____

🍍 Asshole of the Day 🍍

_____
_____
_____
_____
_____
_____
_____

Today, I'm Proud I Didn't...   🍍   Today, I am Happy I Did...

_____   _____
_____   _____
_____   _____
_____   _____
_____   _____
_____   _____

🍍 I'm Lucky To Have 🍍

_____
_____
_____
_____
_____
_____
_____

MY MOOD TODAY (RATED IN PINEAPPLES)

🍍 🍍 🍍 🍍 🍍 🍍 🍍 🍍 🍍 🍍 🍍

> JUST CHUCK IT
> INTO THE
> FUCK IT BUCKET
> AND
> MOVE ON

- ○
- ○
- ○
- ○
- ○
- ○
- ○

Other Shit To Remember

DATE: _____

Asshole of the Day

Today, I'm Proud I Didn't...   Today, I am Happy I Did...

I'm Lucky To Have

MY MOOD TODAY (RATED IN PINEAPPLES)

DRAW SOME SHIT HERE

Today's Shit List
PEOPLE, PLACES OR THINGS

- ○
- ○
- ○
- ○
- ○
- ○
- ○

Other Shit To Remember

DATE: _____

Asshole of the Day

Today, I'm Proud I Didn't...   Today, I am Happy I Did...

I'm Lucky To Have

MY MOOD TODAY (RATED IN PINEAPPLES)

CAPTURE RANDOM FUCKERY HERE

Today's Shit List
PEOPLE, PLACES OR THINGS

- ○
- ○
- ○
- ○
- ○
- ○
- ○

Other Shit To Remember

DATE: _____

Asshole of the Day

_____
_____
_____
_____
_____
_____
_____
_____
_____

Today, I'm Proud I Didn't...   Today, I am Happy I Did...

I'm Lucky To Have

_____
_____
_____
_____
_____
_____

MY MOOD TODAY (RATED IN PINEAPPLES)

WRITE YOUR OWN FUCKING QUOTE

Today's Shit List
PEOPLE, PLACES OR THINGS

Other Shit To Remember

DATE: _____

Asshole of the Day

Today, I'm Proud I Didn't...   Today, I am Happy I Did...

I'm Lucky To Have

MY MOOD TODAY (RATED IN PINEAPPLES)

> **WHEN IN DOUBT, REMEMBER F I S H: 'FUCK IT SHIT HAPPENS'**

- ○
- ○
- ○
- ○
- ○
- ○
- ○

Other Shit To Remember

DATE: _____

Asshole of the Day

_____

Today, I'm Proud I Didn't...   Today, I am Happy I Did...

I'm Lucky To Have

MY MOOD TODAY (RATED IN PINEAPPLES)

DRAW SOME SHIT HERE

Today's Shit List
PEOPLE, PLACES OR THINGS

- ○
- ○
- ○
- ○
- ○
- ○
- ○

Other Shit To Remember

DATE: _____

🍍 Asshole of the Day 🍍

_____

Today, I'm Proud I Didn't... 🍍 Today, I am Happy I Did...

🍍 I'm Lucky To Have 🍍

MY MOOD TODAY (RATED IN PINEAPPLES)

🍍 🍍 🍍 🍍 🍍 🍍 🍍 🍍 🍍 🍍 🍍

CAPTURE RANDOM FUCKERY HERE

Today's Shit List
PEOPLE, PLACES OR THINGS

- ○
- ○
- ○
- ○
- ○
- ○
- ○

Other Shit To Remember

DATE: _____

Asshole of the Day

Today, I'm Proud I Didn't...

Today, I am Happy I Did...

I'm Lucky To Have

MY MOOD TODAY (RATED IN PINEAPPLES)

WRITE YOUR OWN FUCKING QUOTE

Today's Shit List
PEOPLE, PLACES OR THINGS

- ○
- ○
- ○
- ○
- ○
- ○
- ○

Other Shit To Remember

DATE: _____

Asshole of the Day

Today, I'm Proud I Didn't...   _Today, I am Happy I Did..._

I'm Lucky To Have

MY MOOD TODAY (RATED IN PINEAPPLES)

Today's Shit List
PEOPLE, PLACES OR THINGS

- ○
- ○
- ○
- ○
- ○
- ○
- ○

"IT'S BETTER
TO BE
FULL OF WINE
THAN
FULL OF SHIT"

Other Shit To Remember

DATE: _____

Asshole of the Day

_____
_____
_____
_____
_____
_____
_____
_____
_____

Today, I'm Proud I Didn't...   ## Today, I am Happy I Did...

I'm Lucky To Have

_____
_____
_____
_____
_____
_____
_____
_____

MY MOOD TODAY (RATED IN PINEAPPLES)

DRAW SOME SHIT HERE

Today's Shit List
PEOPLE, PLACES OR THINGS

○

○

○

○

○

○

○

Other Shit To Remember

DATE: _____

Asshole of the Day

Today, I'm Proud I Didn't...   Today, I am Happy I Did...

I'm Lucky To Have

MY MOOD TODAY (RATED IN PINEAPPLES)

CAPTURE RANDOM FUCKERY HERE

Today's Shit List
PEOPLE, PLACES OR THINGS

Other Shit To Remember

DATE: _____

🍍 Asshole of the Day 🍍

Today, I'm Proud I Didn't... 🍍 Today, I am Happy I Did...

🍍 I'm Lucky To Have 🍍

MY MOOD TODAY (RATED IN PINEAPPLES)

🍍 🍍 🍍 🍍 🍍 🍍 🍍 🍍 🍍 🍍

WRITE YOUR OWN FUCKING QUOTE

Today's Shit List
PEOPLE, PLACES OR THINGS

Other Shit To Remember

🍍 Asshole of the Day 🍍

Today, I'm Proud I Didn't...   Today, I am Happy I Did...

🍍 I'm Lucky To Have 🍍

MY MOOD TODAY (RATED IN PINEAPPLES)

🍍 🍍 🍍 🍍 🍍 🍍 🍍 🍍 🍍 🍍

"SOMETIMES THE FIRST STEP TO FORGIVENESS IS REALIZING THE PERSON IS A BAT-SHIT CRAZY MOTHERFUCKER"

- ○
- ○
- ○
- ○
- ○
- ○
- ○

Other Shit To Remember

DATE: _____

Asshole of the Day

_____
_____
_____
_____
_____
_____
_____
_____

Today, I'm Proud I Didn't...   Today, I am Happy I Did...

I'm Lucky To Have

_____
_____
_____
_____
_____
_____
_____

MY MOOD TODAY (RATED IN PINEAPPLES)

DRAW SOME SHIT HERE

Today's Shit List
PEOPLE, PLACES OR THINGS

○

○

○

○

○

○

○

Other Shit To Remember

DATE: _____

Asshole of the Day

_____
_____
_____
_____
_____
_____
_____
_____

Today, I'm Proud I Didn't...

_____
_____
_____
_____
_____

Today, I am Happy I Did...

_____
_____
_____
_____
_____

I'm Lucky To Have

_____
_____
_____
_____
_____
_____
_____

MY MOOD TODAY (RATED IN PINEAPPLES)

CAPTURE RANDOM FUCKERY HERE

Today's Shit List
PEOPLE, PLACES OR THINGS

Other Shit To Remember

DATE: _____

Asshole of the Day

Today, I'm Proud I Didn't...   Today, I am Happy I Did...

I'm Lucky To Have

MY MOOD TODAY (RATED IN PINEAPPLES)

WRITE YOUR OWN FUCKING QUOTE

Today's Shit List
PEOPLE, PLACES OR THINGS

- ○
- ○
- ○
- ○
- ○
- ○
- ○

Other Shit To Remember

Asshole of the Day

_____
_____
_____
_____
_____
_____

Today, I'm Proud I Didn't...

_____
_____
_____
_____
_____
_____

Today, I am Happy I Did...

_____
_____
_____
_____
_____
_____

I'm Lucky To Have

_____
_____
_____
_____
_____
_____

MY MOOD TODAY (RATED IN PINEAPPLES)

> "WHAT TIME
> IT IS?
> LOOKS LIKE
> IT'S
> 'FUCK THIS SHIT'
> O'CLOCK"

- ○
- ○
- ○
- ○
- ○
- ○
- ○

Other Shit To Remember

DATE: _____

🍍 Asshole of the Day 🍍

_____
_____
_____
_____
_____
_____
_____

Today, I'm Proud I Didn't...   🍍   Today, I am Happy I Did...

_____   _____
_____   _____
_____   _____
_____   _____
_____   _____
_____   _____

🍍 I'm Lucky To Have 🍍

_____
_____
_____
_____
_____
_____

MY MOOD TODAY (RATED IN PINEAPPLES)

🍍 🍍 🍍 🍍 🍍 🍍 🍍 🍍 🍍 🍍 🍍

CAPTURE RANDOM FUCKERY HERE

Today's Shit List
PEOPLE, PLACES OR THINGS

Other Shit To Remember

DATE: _____

Asshole of the Day

_____

Today, I'm Proud I Didn't...   Today, I am Happy I Did...

I'm Lucky To Have

MY MOOD TODAY (RATED IN PINEAPPLES)

DRAW SOME SHIT HERE

Today's Shit List
PEOPLE, PLACES OR THINGS

- ○
- ○
- ○
- ○
- ○
- ○
- ○

Other Shit To Remember

DATE: _____

Asshole of the Day

_____
_____
_____
_____
_____
_____
_____
_____

Today, I'm Proud I Didn't...

_____
_____
_____
_____
_____
_____

Today, I am Happy I Did...

_____
_____
_____
_____
_____
_____

I'm Lucky To Have

_____
_____
_____
_____
_____
_____
_____

MY MOOD TODAY (RATED IN PINEAPPLES)

Today's Shit List
PEOPLE, PLACES OR THINGS

○
○
○
○
○
○
○

> INHALE
> THE
> GOOD SHIT.
> EXHALE
> THE
> BULLSHIT

Other Shit To Remember

DATE: _____

Asshole of the Day

_____
_____
_____
_____
_____
_____
_____

Today, I'm Proud I Didn't...   Today, I am Happy I Did...

_____   _____
_____   _____
_____   _____
_____   _____
_____   _____
_____   _____

I'm Lucky To Have

_____
_____
_____
_____
_____
_____
_____

MY MOOD TODAY (RATED IN PINEAPPLES)

CAPTURE RANDOM FUCKERY HERE

Today's Shit List
PEOPLE, PLACES OR THINGS

Other Shit To Remember

DATE: _____

Asshole of the Day

Today, I'm Proud I Didn't...

Today, I am Happy I Did...

I'm Lucky To Have

MY MOOD TODAY (RATED IN PINEAPPLES)

WRITE YOUR OWN FUCKING QUOTE

Today's Shit List
PEOPLE, PLACES OR THINGS

- ○
- ○
- ○
- ○
- ○
- ○
- ○

Other Shit To Remember

DATE: _____

Asshole of the Day

_____

Today, I'm Proud I Didn't...   ## Today, I am Happy I Did...

I'm Lucky To Have

MY MOOD TODAY (RATED IN PINEAPPLES)

Today's Shit List
PEOPLE, PLACES OR THINGS

"I'M SMILING BECAUSE I KNOW KARMA WILL BITCH-SLAP YOU EVENTUALLY."

- ○
- ○
- ○
- ○
- ○
- ○
- ○

Other Shit To Remember

DATE: _____

Asshole of the Day

_____
_____
_____
_____
_____
_____
_____
_____
_____

Today, I'm Proud I Didn't...

_____
_____
_____
_____
_____
_____
_____
_____

Today, I am Happy I Did...

_____
_____
_____
_____
_____
_____
_____
_____

I'm Lucky To Have

_____
_____
_____
_____
_____
_____
_____
_____
_____

MY MOOD TODAY (RATED IN PINEAPPLES)

DRAW SOME SHIT HERE

Today's Shit List
PEOPLE, PLACES OR THINGS

○

○

○

○

○

○

○

Other Shit To Remember

DATE: _____

Asshole of the Day

_____

Today, I'm Proud I Didn't...

Today, I am Happy I Did...

_____

I'm Lucky To Have

_____

MY MOOD TODAY (RATED IN PINEAPPLES)

WRITE YOUR OWN FUCKING QUOTE

Today's Shit List
PEOPLE, PLACES OR THINGS

- ○
- ○
- ○
- ○
- ○
- ○
- ○

Other Shit To Remember

DATE: _____

Asshole of the Day

_____
_____
_____
_____
_____
_____
_____

Today, I'm Proud I Didn't...   Today, I am Happy I Did...

_____   _____
_____   _____
_____   _____
_____   _____
_____   _____
_____   _____

I'm Lucky To Have

_____
_____
_____
_____
_____
_____
_____

MY MOOD TODAY (RATED IN PINEAPPLES)

"SOMETIMES I WISH I WAS AN OCTOPUS - SO I COULD SLAP EIGHT PEOPLE AT ONCE."

Other Shit To Remember

DATE: _____

Asshole of the Day

_____
_____
_____
_____
_____
_____
_____
_____
_____

Today, I'm Proud I Didn't...

_____
_____
_____
_____
_____
_____
_____
_____

Today, I am Happy I Did...

_____
_____
_____
_____
_____
_____
_____
_____

I'm Lucky To Have

_____
_____
_____
_____
_____
_____
_____

MY MOOD TODAY (RATED IN PINEAPPLES)

CAPTURE RANDOM FUCKERY HERE

Today's Shit List
PEOPLE, PLACES OR THINGS

- ○
- ○
- ○
- ○
- ○
- ○
- ○

Other Shit To Remember

DATE: _____

Asshole of the Day

_____

Today, I'm Proud I Didn't...

Today, I am Happy I Did...

I'm Lucky To Have

_____

MY MOOD TODAY (RATED IN PINEAPPLES)

DRAW SOME SHIT HERE

Today's Shit List
PEOPLE, PLACES OR THINGS

- ○
- ○
- ○
- ○
- ○
- ○
- ○

Other Shit To Remember

DATE: _____

Asshole of the Day

_____
_____
_____
_____
_____
_____
_____
_____
_____

Today, I'm Proud I Didn't...

_____
_____
_____
_____
_____
_____

Today, I am Happy I Did...

_____
_____
_____
_____
_____
_____

I'm Lucky To Have

_____
_____
_____
_____
_____
_____
_____

MY MOOD TODAY (RATED IN PINEAPPLES)

"
**LITTLE GIRLS
CRY.
BIG GIRLS
SAY
FUCK.**
"

Other Shit To Remember

DATE: _____

Asshole of the Day

Today, I'm Proud I Didn't...

Today, I am Happy I Did...

I'm Lucky To Have

MY MOOD TODAY (RATED IN PINEAPPLES)

DRAW SOME SHIT HERE

Today's Shit List
PEOPLE, PLACES OR THINGS

Other Shit To Remember

DATE: _____

Asshole of the Day

Today, I'm Proud I Didn't...   Today, I am Happy I Did...

I'm Lucky To Have

MY MOOD TODAY (RATED IN PINEAPPLES)

CAPTURE RANDOM FUCKERY HERE

Today's Shit List
PEOPLE, PLACES OR THINGS

Other Shit To Remember

DATE: _____

Asshole of the Day

Today, I'm Proud I Didn't...

Today, I am Happy I Did...

I'm Lucky To Have

MY MOOD TODAY (RATED IN PINEAPPLES)

WRITE YOUR OWN FUCKING QUOTE

Today's Shit List
PEOPLE, PLACES OR THINGS

- ○
- ○
- ○
- ○
- ○
- ○
- ○

Other Shit To Remember

DATE: _____

Asshole of the Day

Today, I'm Proud I Didn't...   _Today, I am Happy I Did..._

I'm Lucky To Have

MY MOOD TODAY (RATED IN PINEAPPLES)

> **I DON'T DO THE CALM THING. I DO THE BREAK SHIT AND SPEW PROFANITY THING.**

Today's Shit List
PEOPLE, PLACES OR THINGS

- ○
- ○
- ○
- ○
- ○
- ○
- ○

Other Shit To Remember

DATE: _____

Asshole of the Day

_____

Today, I'm Proud I Didn't...

_____

Today, I am Happy I Did...

_____

I'm Lucky To Have

_____

MY MOOD TODAY (RATED IN PINEAPPLES)

DRAW SOME SHIT HERE

Today's Shit List
PEOPLE, PLACES OR THINGS

○

○

○

○

○

○

○

Other Shit To Remember

Asshole of the Day

_____
_____
_____
_____
_____
_____
_____
_____

Today, I'm Proud I Didn't...

_____
_____
_____
_____
_____
_____

Today, I am Happy I Did...

_____
_____
_____
_____
_____
_____

I'm Lucky To Have

_____
_____
_____
_____
_____
_____
_____

MY MOOD TODAY (RATED IN PINEAPPLES)

"DON'T HATE
SOMEONE FOR
THEIR OUTSIDE.
HATE THEM
FOR THE
PIECE OF SHIT
THEY ARE INSIDE."

- ○
- ○
- ○
- ○
- ○
- ○
- ○

Other Shit To Remember

DATE: _____

🍍 Asshole of the Day 🍍

_____
_____
_____
_____
_____
_____
_____

Today, I'm Proud I Didn't...   🍍   Today, I am Happy I Did...

_____	_____
_____	_____
_____	_____
_____	_____
_____	_____
_____	_____

🍍 I'm Lucky To Have 🍍

_____
_____
_____
_____
_____
_____
_____

MY MOOD TODAY (RATED IN PINEAPPLES)

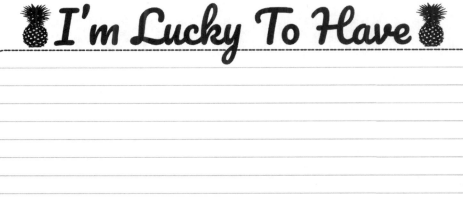

CAPTURE RANDOM FUCKERY HERE

Today's Shit List
PEOPLE, PLACES OR THINGS

- ○
- ○
- ○
- ○
- ○
- ○
- ○

Other Shit To Remember

DATE: _____

Asshole of the Day

_____
_____
_____
_____
_____
_____

Today, I'm Proud I Didn't...

_____
_____
_____
_____
_____
_____

Today, I am Happy I Did...

_____
_____
_____
_____
_____
_____

I'm Lucky To Have

_____
_____
_____
_____
_____

MY MOOD TODAY (RATED IN PINEAPPLES)

> LIFE IS
> SHORT.
> DO LOTS OF
> SHIT
> THAT MATTERS.

Other Shit To Remember

DATE: _____

Asshole of the Day

_____
_____
_____
_____
_____
_____
_____
_____

Today, I'm Proud I Didn't...

_____
_____
_____
_____
_____
_____
_____

Today, I am Happy I Did...

_____
_____
_____
_____
_____
_____
_____

I'm Lucky To Have

_____
_____
_____
_____
_____
_____

MY MOOD TODAY (RATED IN PINEAPPLES)

WRITE YOUR OWN FUCKING QUOTE

Today's Shit List
PEOPLE, PLACES OR THINGS

- ○
- ○
- ○
- ○
- ○
- ○
- ○

Other Shit To Remember

DATE: _____

Asshole of the Day

_____

Today, I'm Proud I Didn't...   ## Today, I am Happy I Did...

I'm Lucky To Have

MY MOOD TODAY (RATED IN PINEAPPLES)

Today's Shit List
PEOPLE, PLACES OR THINGS

> WHEN
> SOMETHING
> GOES
> WRONG IN LIFE,
> YELL
> 'PLOT TWIST, BITCH!'
> AND MOVE ON

- ○
- ○
- ○
- ○
- ○
- ○
- ○

Other Shit To Remember

DATE: _____

Asshole of the Day

_____
_____
_____
_____
_____
_____
_____
_____

Today, I'm Proud I Didn't...

_____
_____
_____
_____
_____
_____
_____

Today, I am Happy I Did...

_____
_____
_____
_____
_____
_____
_____

I'm Lucky To Have

_____
_____
_____
_____
_____
_____
_____

MY MOOD TODAY (RATED IN PINEAPPLES)

DRAW SOME SHIT HERE

Today's Shit List
PEOPLE, PLACES OR THINGS

- ○
- ○
- ○
- ○
- ○
- ○
- ○

Other Shit To Remember

DATE: _____

Asshole of the Day

_____

Today, I'm Proud I Didn't...   Today, I am Happy I Did...

I'm Lucky To Have

MY MOOD TODAY (RATED IN PINEAPPLES)

WRITE YOUR OWN FUCKING QUOTE

Today's Shit List
PEOPLE, PLACES OR THINGS

- ○
- ○
- ○
- ○
- ○
- ○
- ○

Other Shit To Remember

DATE: _____

Asshole of the Day

_____

Today, I'm Proud I Didn't...

Today, I am Happy I Did...

I'm Lucky To Have

MY MOOD TODAY (RATED IN PINEAPPLES)

Today's Shit List
PEOPLE, PLACES OR THINGS

> I WHISPER 'WHAT THE FUCK' TO MYSELF AT LEAST 50 TIMES A DAY TO SURVIVE THIS SHIT.

- ○
- ○
- ○
- ○
- ○
- ○
- ○

Other Shit To Remember

DATE: _____

Asshole of the Day

_____
_____
_____
_____
_____
_____
_____
_____

Today, I'm Proud I Didn't...

_____
_____
_____
_____
_____
_____
_____
_____

Today, I am Happy I Did...

_____
_____
_____
_____
_____
_____
_____
_____

I'm Lucky To Have

_____
_____
_____
_____
_____
_____
_____
_____

MY MOOD TODAY (RATED IN PINEAPPLES)

CAPTURE RANDOM FUCKERY HERE

Today's Shit List
PEOPLE, PLACES OR THINGS

Other Shit To Remember

DATE: _____

Asshole of the Day

_____

Today, I'm Proud I Didn't...   Today, I am Happy I Did...

I'm Lucky To Have

MY MOOD TODAY (RATED IN PINEAPPLES)

"I SMILE ON
THE OUTSIDE...
BUT AM
SCREAMING
'YOU'RE AN
ASSHOLE'
ON THE INSIDE"

Other Shit To Remember

DATE: _____

Asshole of the Day

_____
_____
_____
_____
_____
_____
_____
_____
_____

Today, I'm Proud I Didn't...   ## Today, I am Happy I Did...

_____   _____
_____   _____
_____   _____
_____   _____
_____   _____
_____   _____
_____   _____

I'm Lucky To Have

_____
_____
_____
_____
_____
_____
_____
_____

MY MOOD TODAY (RATED IN PINEAPPLES)

DRAW SOME SHIT HERE

Today's Shit List
PEOPLE, PLACES OR THINGS

- ○
- ○
- ○
- ○
- ○
- ○
- ○

Other Shit To Remember

DATE: _____

Asshole of the Day

Today, I'm Proud I Didn't...   Today, I am Happy I Did...

I'm Lucky To Have

MY MOOD TODAY (RATED IN PINEAPPLES)

Today's Shit List
PEOPLE, PLACES OR THINGS

○
○
○
○
○
○
○

"IF YOU
MUST CURSE,
PLEASE USE
YOUR OWN NAME.
~GOD"

Other Shit To Remember

DATE: _____

Asshole of the Day

Today, I'm Proud I Didn't...   Today, I am Happy I Did...

I'm Lucky To Have

MY MOOD TODAY (RATED IN PINEAPPLES)

CAPTURE RANDOM FUCKERY HERE

Today's Shit List
PEOPLE, PLACES OR THINGS

Other Shit To Remember

DATE: _____

Asshole of the Day

_____
_____
_____
_____
_____
_____
_____
_____

Today, I'm Proud I Didn't...   Today, I am Happy I Did...

_____	_____
_____	_____
_____	_____
_____	_____
_____	_____
_____	_____
_____	_____

I'm Lucky To Have

_____
_____
_____
_____
_____
_____
_____
_____

MY MOOD TODAY (RATED IN PINEAPPLES)

Today's Shit List
PEOPLE, PLACES OR THINGS

- ○
- ○
- ○
- ○
- ○
- ○
- ○

"
I USED
MANNERS TODAY.
I SAID
'BITCH, PLEASE'.
IT COUNTS.
"

Other Shit To Remember

DATE: _____

🍍 Asshole of the Day 🍍

_____
_____
_____
_____
_____
_____
_____
_____

Today, I'm Proud I Didn't... 🍍 Today, I am Happy I Did...

_____	_____
_____	_____
_____	_____
_____	_____
_____	_____
_____	_____
_____	_____

🍍 I'm Lucky To Have 🍍

_____
_____
_____
_____
_____
_____
_____

MY MOOD TODAY (RATED IN PINEAPPLES)

🍍 🍍 🍍 🍍 🍍 🍍 🍍 🍍 🍍 🍍 🍍

WRITE YOUR OWN FUCKING QUOTE

Today's Shit List
PEOPLE, PLACES OR THINGS

- ○
- ○
- ○
- ○
- ○
- ○
- ○

Other Shit To Remember

DATE: _____

Asshole of the Day

(lined writing area)

Today, I'm Proud I Didn't...   Today, I am Happy I Did...

(two lined writing areas)

I'm Lucky To Have

(lined writing area)

MY MOOD TODAY (RATED IN PINEAPPLES)

> "GROW UP,
> BE A UNICORN,
> STAB PEOPLE
> WITH YOUR
> HEAD.

- ○
- ○
- ○
- ○
- ○
- ○
- ○

Other Shit To Remember

DATE: _____

Asshole of the Day

_____
_____
_____
_____
_____
_____
_____
_____

Today, I'm Proud I Didn't...

_____
_____
_____
_____
_____
_____
_____

Today, I am Happy I Did...

_____
_____
_____
_____
_____
_____
_____

I'm Lucky To Have

_____
_____
_____
_____
_____
_____
_____

MY MOOD TODAY (RATED IN PINEAPPLES)

DRAW SOME SHIT HERE

Today's Shit List
PEOPLE, PLACES OR THINGS

○
○
○
○
○
○
○

Other Shit To Remember

DATE: _____

Asshole of the Day

_____
_____
_____
_____
_____
_____
_____
_____

Today, I'm Proud I Didn't...

_____
_____
_____
_____
_____
_____

Today, I am Happy I Did...

_____
_____
_____
_____
_____
_____

I'm Lucky To Have

_____
_____
_____
_____
_____
_____

MY MOOD TODAY (RATED IN PINEAPPLES)

WRITE YOUR OWN FUCKING QUOTE

Today's Shit List
PEOPLE, PLACES OR THINGS

- ○
- ○
- ○
- ○
- ○
- ○
- ○

Other Shit To Remember

DATE: _____

Asshole of the Day

_____
_____
_____
_____
_____
_____
_____

Today, I'm Proud I Didn't...

_____
_____
_____
_____
_____
_____
_____

Today, I am Happy I Did...

_____
_____
_____
_____
_____
_____
_____

I'm Lucky To Have

_____
_____
_____
_____
_____
_____

MY MOOD TODAY (RATED IN PINEAPPLES)

"I ACT LIKE A
LADY.
I CURSE
LIKE A SAILOR.
WHAT'S YOUR
FUCKING PROBLEM
WITH THAT?"

-
-
-
-
-
-
-

Other Shit To Remember

DATE: _____

Asshole of the Day

_____
_____
_____
_____
_____
_____
_____
_____

Today, I'm Proud I Didn't...

Today, I am Happy I Did...

I'm Lucky To Have

_____
_____
_____
_____
_____
_____
_____

MY MOOD TODAY (RATED IN PINEAPPLES)

CAPTURE RANDOM
FUCKERY HERE

Today's Shit List
PEOPLE, PLACES OR THINGS

- ○
- ○
- ○
- ○
- ○
- ○
- ○

Other Shit To Remember

DATE: _____

🍍 Asshole of the Day 🍍

_____

Today, I'm Proud I Didn't... 🍍 Today, I am Happy I Did...

🍍 I'm Lucky To Have 🍍

_____

MY MOOD TODAY (RATED IN PINEAPPLES)

🍍 🍍 🍍 🍍 🍍 🍍 🍍 🍍 🍍 🍍 🍍

Today's Shit List
PEOPLE, PLACES OR THINGS

"DON'T LET ANYONE WITH UGLY SHOES TELL YOU SHIT ABOUT LIFE."

- ○
- ○
- ○
- ○
- ○
- ○
- ○

Other Shit To Remember

DATE: _____

Asshole of the Day

_____
_____
_____
_____
_____
_____
_____
_____
_____

Today, I'm Proud I Didn't...

_____
_____
_____
_____
_____
_____

Today, I am Happy I Did...

_____
_____
_____
_____
_____
_____

I'm Lucky To Have

_____
_____
_____
_____
_____
_____
_____
_____

MY MOOD TODAY (RATED IN PINEAPPLES)

DRAW SOME SHIT HERE

Today's Shit List
PEOPLE, PLACES OR THINGS

- ○
- ○
- ○
- ○
- ○
- ○
- ○

Other Shit To Remember

DATE: _____

Asshole of the Day

Today, I'm Proud I Didn't...

Today, I am Happy I Did...

I'm Lucky To Have

MY MOOD TODAY (RATED IN PINEAPPLES)

"IT'S OKAY
IF YOU
DON'T LIKE ME.
NOT EVERYONE
HAS
GOOD TASTE."

Other Shit To Remember

DATE: _____

Asshole of the Day

_____

Today, I'm Proud I Didn't...   ## Today, I am Happy I Did...

I'm Lucky To Have

MY MOOD TODAY (RATED IN PINEAPPLES)

DRAW SOME SHIT HERE

Today's Shit List
PEOPLE, PLACES OR THINGS

- ○
- ○
- ○
- ○
- ○
- ○
- ○

Other Shit To Remember

DATE: _____

Asshole of the Day

_____
_____
_____
_____
_____
_____
_____
_____

Today, I'm Proud I Didn't...

_____
_____
_____
_____
_____
_____
_____
_____

Today, I am Happy I Did...

_____
_____
_____
_____
_____
_____
_____
_____

I'm Lucky To Have

_____
_____
_____
_____
_____
_____
_____
_____

MY MOOD TODAY (RATED IN PINEAPPLES)

DRAW SOME SHIT HERE

Today's Shit List
PEOPLE, PLACES OR THINGS

- ○
- ○
- ○
- ○
- ○
- ○
- ○

Other Shit To Remember

THE CRAZY TIRED BEETCHES™ STORY

Crazy Tired Beetches™ is a small, woman-owned company that publishes unique and fun planners, journals and gifts. We believe that cuss words can make you happy, and we are simply a group of women who enjoy laughing at life.

Our journals, planners and calendars are designed for women to pick up, giggle, and share a laugh with their friends, family and colleagues. We are a little bit snarky, a little bit sassy, and a whole lot of fun!

We may cuss (a TON), but we find sometimes a few strategically placed F-Bombs make the stress and insanity of everyday life laughable, and a heck of a lot more enjoyable!

With that, we hope you find a giggle, belly laugh or just smile at our collection of products. If you do, we would love it if you would leave us a review on Amazon!

We are proudly based in the USA and look forward to continuing taking life not too seriously with you!

~Sending love from the CTB crew!

www.crazytiredbeetches.com